AUSTRALIA'S SCARIEST CREATURES

BY JOHN LESLEY

FREAKY INSECTS

REDBACK publishing

First published 2024 by
Redback Publishing
PO Box 357 Frenchs Forest NSW 2086
Australia

www.redbackpublishing.com
orders@redbackpublishing.com

ISBN 978-1-761400-40-7

Author: John Lesley
Editor: Caroline Thomas
Designer: Redback Publishing
Original illustrations © Redback Publishing 2024
Originated by Redback Publishing

Abbreviations: l—left, r—right, b—bottom, t—top, c—centre, m—middle
We would like to thank the following for permission to reproduce photographs: Shutterstock; p8bl Kgbo, CC BY-SA 4.0 (https://creativecommons.org/licenses/by-sa/4.0>, via Wikimedia Commons); p14-15 m Bernard DUPONT from FRANCE, CC BY-SA 2.0 (https://creativecommons.org/licenses/by-sa/2.0), via Wikimedia Commons; p 17tl Donald Hobern, CC BY 2.0 (https://creativecommons.org/licenses/by/2.0), via Wikimedia Commons); p20-21c fStop Images GmbH/Alamy Stock Photo; p21bl Mark Marathon, CC BY-SA 3.0 (https://creativecommons.org/licenses/by-sa/3.0), via Wikimedia Commons, p24tl Wildan ardani, CC BY-SA 4.0 (https://creativecommons.org/licenses/by-sa/4.0), via Wikimedia Commons, 31br bogong moth, John Tann, flicker.com, https://www.flickr.com/photos/31031835@N08/10301606615

NATIONAL LIBRARY OF AUSTRALIA
A catalogue record for this book is available from the National Library of Australia

CONTENTS

BULLDOG ANT

Myrmecia

Bulldog ants are easily angered, very aggressive, and their bite is excruciating. Once one of them bites, it sends out a signal by releasing a smell that tells all of the others to converge and start biting as well. Stand on a bulldog ant nest by mistake in the bush, and you will soon realise your mistake. One bite is painful but not deadly unless you are allergic to them. Multiple bites can be very dangerous.

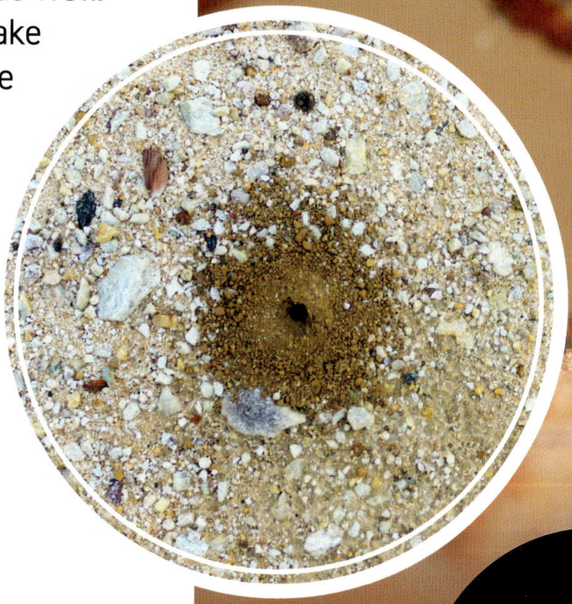

Bulldog ants grow to over four centimetres long. Their jaws are large and their bodies are black and orange. They build their nests very deep underground and with multiple chambers.

They pile up large mounds of dirt, up to a metre across, on top of their nest. There are lookout ants posted at the opening and they will let the others underground know if any living thing comes too close. Then they will all swarm out and attack.

If two queen ants encounter each other, they will fight to the death to rule the colony.

FACT

There is one queen ant in the nest. Her only role is to lay eggs, and all the other ants look after her with great care.

FACT

When it attacks, the bulldog ant will hold on with its jaws, then twist its abdomen around to insert its stinger.

GIANT COCKROACH

Macropanesthia rhinoceros

The Australian giant, burrowing cockroach will sit happily in the palm of your hand, rather than scuttling off like the faster cockroaches that live in our kitchens. It has a segmented body that is glossy brown, and it can grow up to ten centimetres long. Just the thought of touching such a large cockroach would horrify some people.

The giant cockroach lives in leaf litter in forests and does not want to take up residence in people's homes. It does not bite or spread germs. It has an important role in its habitat, eating decaying plant matter to recycle it. They have a flat, oval shape, which makes it easy for them to move through dead plant material and leaves on the ground.

The female gives birth to little cockroaches, rather than laying eggs like most insects do. The young are called nymphs, and they stay in the female's underground burrow until they are old enough to look after themselves. The burrow can extend for a metre down into the ground.

FACT

Giant cockroaches are native to Australia, adding to the long list of big and scary wildlife that lives there.

Also called the rhinoceros cockroach.

FACT

Giant cockroaches can suffer with obesity if they do not move around enough.

STICK INSECT

Ctenomorpha gargantua

The biggest stick insect in Australia is extremely rare. It looks like a small branch, until it moves. They can be over half a metre long, but they are not dangerous and will not chase you. If one does land on you by mistake, move it very gently to a nearby tree, where both you and it will be happier. Their claws can be sharp and scratchy, so move slowly and carefully if you need to dislodge one from yourself.

Never harm a stick insect, as they are not out to attack you and actually make good pets. Like all native animals, they should not be taken from the wild. Buy yours at a specialised pet shop instead.

Stick insects have wings and can fly, which can be very startling for a human who is getting too close. Seeing what looks like a metre-long branch suddenly starting to fly away, and making a lot of rustling noise at the same time, can be scary.

FACT

Stick insects sway slightly so they look more like a twig moving in the breeze.

FACT

Stick insects are called phasmids. They are mostly very rare, but sometimes breed in plague numbers and can destroy trees.

FACT

Some female stick insects can produce eggs without needing a male to fertilise them.

SPINY LEAF INSECT

The spiny leaf insect looks just like a bunch of brown leaves. When it stretches itself out it is up to twenty centimetres long. Its legs, tail and body segments are all shaped like brown leaves. In the bush, you can be right next to one of these big insects and not see it until it moves.

They are not harmful, and some people handle them and keep them as pets. Having such a big insect sitting on your hand can be very intimidating for some people, and it is difficult to overcome the urge to violently shake it off. Try not to do this if you are lucky enough to encounter a spiny leaf insect, as they are harmless and easily injured. Put your hand near a tree, and the insect will usually be glad to slowly climb away.

FACT

Spiny leaf insects do have little spikes on their legs, and these may cause a scratching feeling on your hand.

Spiny leaf insects are phasmids, like stick insects, but they look like leaves instead of twigs.

FACT

The female lays many small, dark grey eggs that drop to the forest floor, where they can last for a long time before they hatch.

CICADA-KILLER WASP

Exeirus lateritius

Unless provoked, the cicada-killer wasps do not normally attack people.

Wasps have a bad reputation for getting angry and stinging, but the habits and size of the cicada-killer wasp make it even more terrifying. They hunt and attack cicadas, which they sting and paralyse, but don't kill. After stinging it, the wasp struggles to drag its paralysed prey along the ground and into its burrow. The female lays an egg on or near the fresh cicada, so that the young wasp has living food to eat when it hatches out.

The wasp grows up to five centimetres long, and is the usual black, yellow and brown colour that many wasps have. Although they live in bushland, they also hunt in suburban areas near people, mostly on the east coast of Australia.

FACT

The entrance to the underground tunnel of a cicada-killer wasp can be a few centimetres wide, and the burrow can be mistaken for the home of a small lizard or other harmless creature.

FACT

These killer wasps look for the fattest cicadas to ensure the wasp grub is well-fed.

ZOMBIE ANTS

The *Cordyceps* fungus can turn ordinary ants into real-life zombies.

FACT

The zombie ant is powerless to resist once the fungus has taken over its brain.

The *Cordyceps* fungus is a predator that gets inside an ant and takes over its behaviour. The fungus controls what the ant does, forcing it to go to a place where there is a suitable temperature for the fungus to thrive. The fungus grows inside the ant until it can eventually make a hole and poke out of the ant's head, or other part of the ant's body. The spores of the fungus can then be released, and they float off to infect other ants, turning them into zombies as well. After they are no longer useful as food and a means of transport for the fungus, the zombie ant dies.

FACT

If the other ants see a zombie ant in the nest, they carry it away and dump it outside.

FACT

The *Cordyceps* fungus can also infect other types of insects, turning them all into zombies.

PROCESSIONARY CATERPILLARS

Ochrogaster lunifer

Covered in hairs that sting if you touch them, processionary caterpillars move about in large, stinging groups, searching for food.

They look as though they are covered in soft, grey hairs, but never touch one or you will regret it. The hairs are very hard to remove from your skin and will stick into you, continuing to sting and causing a lot of pain. Rubbing these hairs into your eyes can be disastrous.

Processionary caterpillars are the caterpillar stage of bag moths, and they usually like to live on wattle trees. They will travel in search of food, all moving together in lines that can be many metres long. They can also be found all spiralled together in a massive stinging bunch. Keep well away!

FACT

The caterpillars turn into moths that are also covered in stinging hairs.

FACT

Take care if investigating a strange, big lump on or under a wattle tree - it might be a group of resting hairy caterpillars.

Just being near these caterpillars is dangerous since their hairs can blow off in the wind.

HERCULES MOTH

Coscinocera hercules

The Hercules moth is enormous, with a wingspan up to thirty centimetres wide. They are brown, black and white, which camouflages them on branches when they are not moving. The body is covered in hair that looks like fur.

Hercules moths are not harmful to humans, so just enjoy the sight of one flying off if you get the chance. To move a Hercules moth outside if it has flown into a room, gently guide it through an open door or window with a large piece of cardboard. Some people are terrified of large flying insects, but these moths are not harmful if they land on you. Sadly, as with many large moths and butterflies, the Hercules moth is not as common as it once was, due to environmental pollution, pesticides and the loss of its bushland habitat.

FACT

The larvae are pale blue with bright, yellow spikes, and grow to over ten centimetres long.

FACT

The adult moths have no mouthparts and so cannot eat. They live for less than two weeks.

FACT

The wings of the adults have transparent patches on them, like little windows.

WITCHETTY GRUB

Endoxyla leucomochla

FACT

Also called a cossid wood moth grub.

Witchetty grubs are a well-known bush food in Australia, where Indigenous people have been roasting and eating them for thousands of years. Today, adventurous restaurants will include witchetty grubs on their menu. The term witchetty grub is sometimes used to describe other sorts of big, white grubs of moths and beetles.

The moth eggs hatch into witchetty grubs, or larvae, that like to feed on the roots of an acacia tree called a witchetty bush. When they are ready to pupate, the grubs stop eating and create a protective cocoon as they undergo a change into a moth. The adult moth has the colouring of tree bark.

FACT

This moth can grow to have a wingspan of over fifteen centimetres.

FACT

Witchetty grubs live in burrows under trees, where they eat the roots.

The adult moth breaks out of its pupa and must wait a few minutes for its wings to fill with fluid before it can fly. The moth's only purpose after reaching this part of the lifecycle is to find a mate and breed. Then they die.

At this adult stage of life, the moths have no mouth or biting parts, so they are not harmful to humans. These huge moths used to be common, even in the suburbs, but the advancing development of towns and the resultant removal of trees have contributed to a decrease in their numbers.

RHINOCEROS BEETLE

Xylotrupes ulysses

FACT

Although the male beetle's horn makes it look intimidating, these beetles are not at all harmful to humans.

The black rhinoceros beetle is Australia's biggest beetle, and it lives in the warm and tropical parts of Australia. Glossy black or brown, strong and formidable, the male has horns on its large head and thorax, and it uses them to fight with other males. The smaller females do not grow horns, making them look like big Christmas beetles, to which they are related.

Rhinoceros beetles can grow up to seven centimetres long. The larvae, or grubs, are just as big. They eat rotting plant material and are sometimes found in suburban compost bins, although the forest floor is their natural habitat. After pupating under the ground, the beetle emerges. It is an omnivore, eating plants as well as dead animals. They particularly like to eat the leaves of Poinciana trees.

Rhinoceros beetles hiss when they are fighting, or if you pick one up.

FACT

The sturdy exoskeleton enables the males to knock each other over when fighting.

ASSASSIN FLIES

FACT

Assassin flies have a long, thin abdomen and very large eyes.

Bush flies are common in Australia and are very annoying, but there is one type of fly that is more than just an annoyance. Assassin flies are aggressive hunters, eating other insects that they catch while flying. They grab prey with the claws on the ends of their legs, then inject it with a poison that starts to dissolve the internal organs. The assassin fly larvae are also carnivorous, looking for soft foods such as other larvae or insect eggs. Assassin flies make us think of flies in a whole new way!

They can grow up to three centimetres long, which is big for a fly. They have a variety of habitats and are most numerous in regions with a warm and humid climate.

Assassin flies are also called robber flies.

FACT

Assassin flies can use their strong mouthparts to bite humans, but they do not see us as food.

HOW ARE INSECTS SPECIAL?

Insects are in the animal group Arthropoda, which includes crabs, lobsters, centipedes and spiders.

WHAT IS DIFFERENT ABOUT INSECTS?

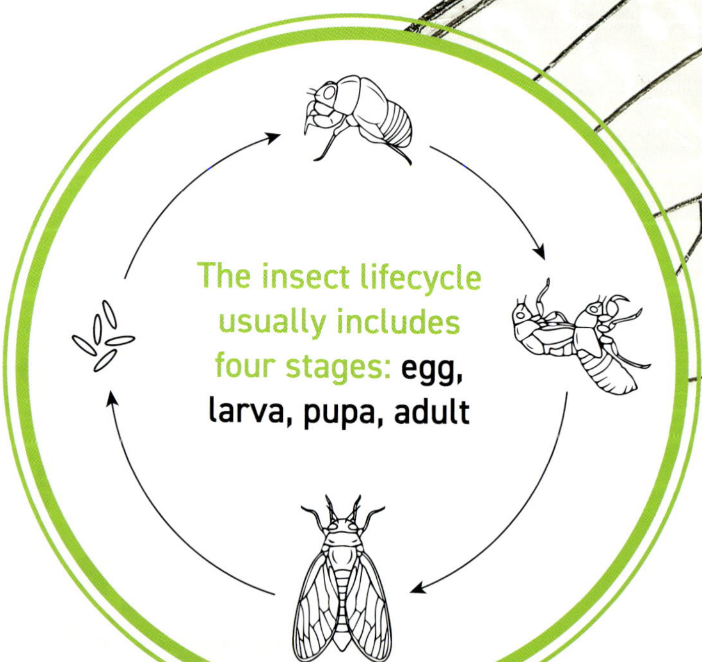

There are two sensory **antennae** on the head

Insects are the only invertebrates that have **wings** and can fly

Instead of internal bones, insects have a hard shell called an **exoskeleton** that gives them their shape. Insects need to shed this hard skin as they grow bigger

The adult form has **six legs**

The three body parts are: **head, thorax, abdomen**

CREEPY CRAWLY PETS

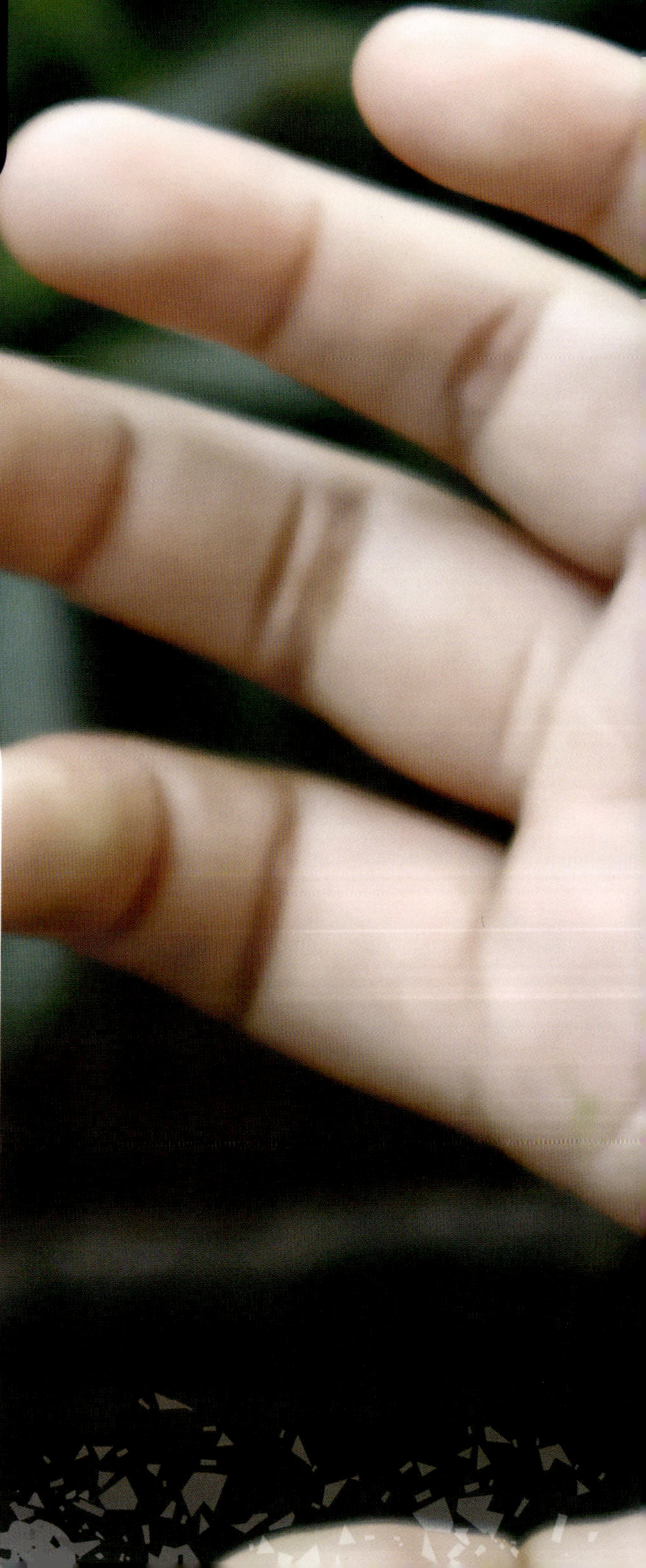

Fear of creepy crawlies is very common and stops many people from ever considering keeping insects as pets.

If you want a pet that likes cuddles and welcomes you when you get home, then an insect is not for you. If you are fascinated by these small but impressive creatures, then keeping a pet insect can be one of the most interesting things you can do.

Insects are good at escaping from cages and disappearing somewhere into the house. They need special diets and conditions to survive, so you will need to do some research before even thinking about keeping a creepy crawly.

As with all native creatures, never take an insect from the wild. You should seek a specialised insect pet seller instead.

QUESTION & ANSWER

?

Why are there no huge insects, like the ones in science fiction movies?

A: The hard exoskeleton restricts the size to which an insect can grow, without all its internal organs collapsing.

AUSTRALIAN SPINY LEAF STICK INSECT

MORE OF AUSTRALIA'S MANY INSECTS

SHIELD BUG
LADY BIRD
DRAGONFLY
PRAYING MANTIS
BOGONG MOTH
CHRISTMAS BEETLE

GLOSSARY

Insect Word List

excruciating very painful

exoskeleton external body support

fertilise action by a male animal that causes an egg to grow into a new individual

formidable frightening and powerful

intimidating frightening

nymph juvenile insect

obesity condition of being overweight

paralyse cause to be unable to move

pupate go into a condition in which all the insect's body parts change

INDEX